D0567574

MARCH
PATTERNS, PROJECTS & PLANS

by
Imogene Forte

Incentive Publications, Inc.
Nashville, Tennessee

Illustrated by Marta Johnson
Cover by Susan Eaddy
Edited by Sally Sharpe

ISBN 0-86530-138-7

Table of Contents

PREFACE

March – a month of wind and fun!

MARCH...

...A TIME of shamrocks and leprechauns — green shamrocks decorate classrooms and homemade cards, children dream of leprechauns and three wishes, classes celebrate the 17th with parties and "green" refreshments, and everyone wears green for good luck!

...A TIME of whistling winds — colorful kites dance overhead, paper airplanes and other flying toys soar through the sky, children run and play, and trees sway as gentle breezes blow.

...A TIME of seasonal change — the last snow melts away as signs of spring appear, warm winds blow, trees and flowers begin to bud and blossom, and the first day of spring finally arrives!

All of this and more is the excitement of March! Watch students' smiles widen and their eyes brighten as your "come alive" classroom says "March is here!" from the ceiling to the floor, from windows and doors, from work sheets and activity projects, from stories and books, and especially from you — an enthusiastic, "project planned" teacher.

This little book of MARCH PATTERNS, PROJECTS & PLANS has been put together with tender loving care to help you be prepared to meet every one of the school days in March with special treats, learning projects and fun surprises that will make your students eager to participate in every phase of the daily schedule and look forward to the next day. Best of all, the patterns, projects and plans are ready for quick and easy use and require no elaborate materials and very little advance preparation.

For your convenience, the materials in this book have been organized around three major unit themes. Each of the patterns, projects and plans can be used independently of the unit plan, however, to be just as effective in classrooms in which teachers choose not to use a unit approach. All are planned to complement and enrich adopted curriculum schemes and to meet young children's interests and learning needs.

Major unit themes include:

- Marvelous March
- Leaping Leprechauns
- It's Our World

Each unit includes a major objective and things to do; poster/booklet cover, bulletin board or display; patterns; art and/or an assembly project; reproducible basic skills activities; and book, story and poem suggestions to make the literature connection.

Other topics, special days and events for which patterns, projects and plans have been provided include:

- Wind & Weather
- Pretending & Make-Believe

MARVELOUS MARCH

Major Objective:
Children will develop awareness of the colors, sights, sounds and special events that characterize the month of March.

Things To Do:

- Use the patterns in this book to make decorations for doors, windows, desks, etc.

- Mark the end of winter and the arrival of spring by helping the children create "winter to spring" pictures. Distribute large sheets of drawing paper and crayons. Discuss with the children the changes that can be observed during March. Ask the children to fold the drawing paper in half and to print *winter* on one side and *spring* on the other (or use the snowman and sun symbols on page 24). Have the children select three crayons to use for each scene. Encourage them to show as many details as possible. Display the pictures on a bulletin board or "clothes line" and discuss the illustrated changes as they can be observed during the month.

- Celebrate one of the last, bleak days of winter with an early morning surprise of hot chocolate and marshmallows. Ask the children to name words that describe hot chocolate as you write them on a chart. Help the children to make up short stories or poems using the words (e.g. "Hot chocolate is yummy; it feels good in my tummy.")

- Send the "letter to parents" (page 10) home to announce the month's activities and to ask for donations for your materials collection. Check your supplies to be sure that you are ready for the month!

To complete the activities in this book, you will need:

construction paper (assorted colors)	green yarn
crayons & markers	index cards
paste	ribbon
tape	materials for vivarium (pg. 64)
scissors	materials for "garbage can
stapler	garden" (pg. 76)
pencils	
drawing paper	
tacks or straight pins	
materials for weather vane (pg. 30)	
materials for recipes (pg.44)	

Dear Parents,

The month of March brings shamrocks, leprechauns, hot-air balloons, weather vanes, fairy tales, nursery rhymes, wildlife and nature into our classroom. This month we will celebrate and learn about St. Patrick's Day, March wind, make-believe and pantomime, wildlife, natural resources and much more.

Your child will bring home artwork, recipes, stories, papers and other special projects to share with you. Your encouragement and reinforcement will boost your child's self-esteem as well as help to stimulate future creative development and learning curiosity.

You may help with our monthly projects by collecting and contributing good "act out" books, stories and rhymes; pictures of animals in their natural environments and wildlife magazines; and throw-away food items such as avocado seeds and pineapple "tops" for growing "garbage can gardens."

This month promises to have many rewarding learning experiences for our class. We hope you will share in those experiences with us!

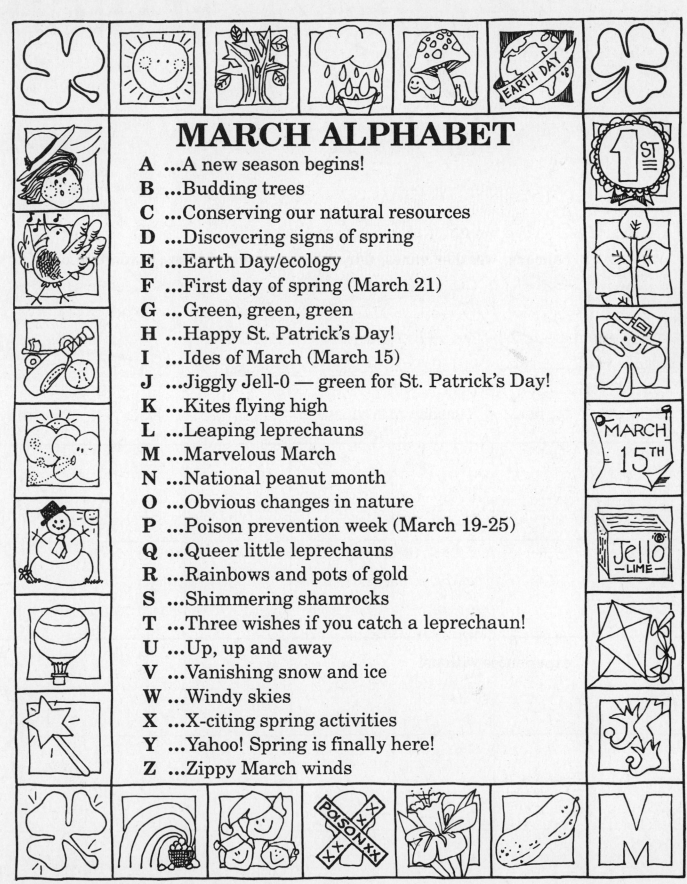

MARCH ALPHABET

A ...A new season begins!
B ...Budding trees
C ...Conserving our natural resources
D ...Discovering signs of spring
E ...Earth Day/ecology
F ...First day of spring (March 21)
G ...Green, green, green
H ...Happy St. Patrick's Day!
I ...Ides of March (March 15)
J ...Jiggly Jell-0 — green for St. Patrick's Day!
K ...Kites flying high
L ...Leaping leprechauns
M ...Marvelous March
N ...National peanut month
O ...Obvious changes in nature
P ...Poison prevention week (March 19-25)
Q ...Queer little leprechauns
R ...Rainbows and pots of gold
S ...Shimmering shamrocks
T ...Three wishes if you catch a leprechaun!
U ...Up, up and away
V ...Vanishing snow and ice
W ...Windy skies
X ...X-citing spring activities
Y ...Yahoo! Spring is finally here!
Z ...Zippy March winds

MARCH

Sunday	Monday	Tuesday	Wednesday	Thursday	Friday	Saturday

HOW TO USE THE MARCH CALENDAR

Use the calendar to:

... find on what day of the week the first day of March falls
... count the number of days in March
... find the number on the calendar which represents March
... mark the birthdays of "March babies" in your room
... mark special days

- St. Patrick's Day (March 17)
- National Poison Prevention Week (March 19-25)
- Earth Day (March 21)
- First Day of spring (March 21)
- etc.

CALENDAR ART

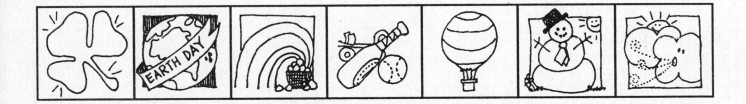

MARCH MANAGEMENT CHART

CLASSROOM HELPERS

My name is

Name Tag

Teacher's Helper

CLEAN ENVIRONMENT AWARD

To: _____

Lucky Leprechaun Award

To: _____

SHAMROCK SHOW-OFF

To "show off" good work, help the children color and cut out shamrock show-offs to attach to their papers. Show-offs make attractive bulletin board displays and great "take homes"!

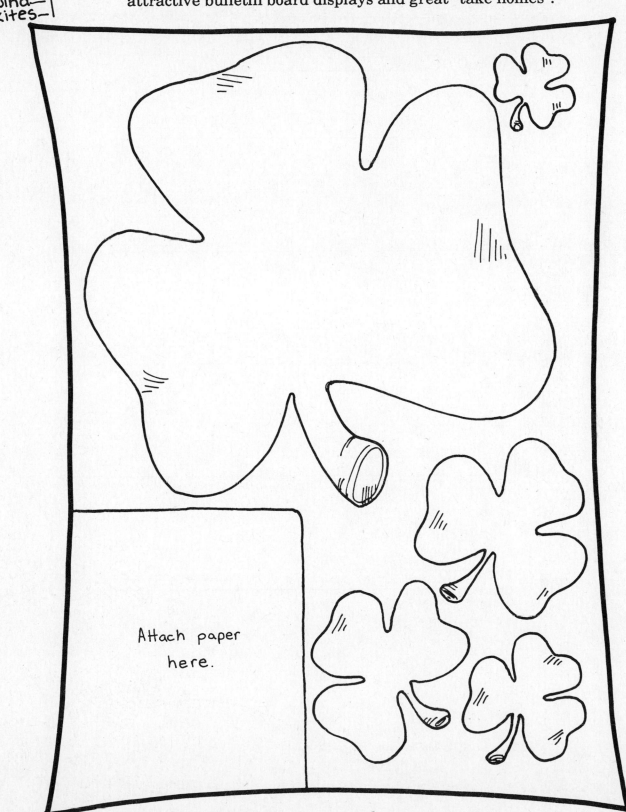

Attach paper here.

Here's what's happening in our Classroom!

Week of _____

Monday _____

Tuesday _____

Wednesday_____

Thursday _____

Friday _____

BLOW, WIND, BLOW

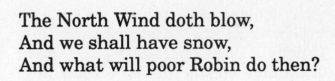

Blow, wind, blow! and go, mill, go!
That the miller may grind his corn;
That the baker may take it,
And into rolls make it,
And send us some hot in the morn.

The North Wind doth blow,
And we shall have snow,
And what will poor Robin do then?

He will hop to a barn,
And to keep himself warm,
Will hide his head under his wing,
   Poor thing!

When the wind is in the east,
'Tis neither good for man nor beast.
When the wind is in the north,
The skillful fisher goes not forth.
When the wind is in the south,
It blows the bait in the fisher's mouth.
When the wind is in the west,
Then 'tis at the very best.

Mother Goose rhymes
© 1990 by Incentive Publications, Inc., Nashville, TN.

WHO HAS SEEN THE WIND?

- Since March weather is characterized by blustery winds and sudden weather changes, it is a perfect month for daily weather prediction, observation and discussion. Construct the bulletin  board on page 27 and attach the children's work to the board for display.

- Construct the bulletin board on page 21 and introduce it to the children on the first school day in March. Explain that the saying "In like a lion and out like a lamb" has been used for generations to express that March usually begins with cold weather, high winds, and rain storms, but ends with warmer weather, soft winds and budding trees and flowers.

- Invite a meteorologist from a local T.V. or radio station to visit the class to discuss his or her responsibilities. Help the children develop a list of questions to ask the visitor before he or she arrives. Have the children draw "weather pictures" to give to the visitor with a thank-you note after the visit. If a meteorologist is not available, bring a T.V. or radio to class and let the children listen to a weather forecast each morning.

- Reproduce and cut out a supply of weather prediction symbols (page 26). Place the symbols near the weather calendar (page 25). Each morning, discuss the weather and pin a wind symbol on the calendar if the children think that the day will be windy. The next morning, discuss the  prediction made the previous day. If the children predicted wind and their prediction was correct (even if it was windy for only a short time), leave the wind symbol on the calendar. If it was not windy, replace the wind symbol with a "we missed" symbol. If the children predicted there would be no wind and their prediction was incorrect, add a "we missed" symbol. At the end of the month it will be fun to see how successful the class was at predicting the weather!

- Read Gilberto and the Wind (see page 78).

- To help the children understand the directions north, south, east and west, let them help to make a weather vane (page 30). Have the children play the game on page 31 to reinforce the experience.

- Read the Mother Goose rhymes on page 19 to the class and use them for choral reading and creative movement projects.

Construction:

1. Reproduce the lion and lamb patterns on pages 22 and 23 and color them with markers or cut them out of construction paper.

2. Reproduce the March weather symbols on page 24 and have the children cut them out and color them with crayons or markers.

3. Reproduce the calendar on page 25 and attach it to the center of the board.

4. Cut the caption "March — In Like A Lion & Out Like A Lamb" out of construction paper.

5. Assemble the board as shown. Have the children pin the March weather symbols on the appropriate sides of the board.

LION

LAMB

MARCH WEATHER SYMBOLS

Sunday	Monday	Tuesday	Wednesday	Thursday	Friday	Saturday

WEATHER PREDICTION SYMBOLS

Construction:

1. Cover the board with blue construction paper or butcher paper.
2. Enlarge the hot-air balloon pattern (page 28) and color it with markers or cut it out of construction paper. Attach it to a corner of the board as shown.
3. Have the children use crayons or tempera paint to "draw" background scenery on the board. (Your supervision will be needed!)
4. Have the children complete the activity on page 29. Display the completed work sheets on the board.
5. Reproduce page 26 for each child and instruct the children to cut wind symbols out of construction paper to add to the board.
6. Cut the caption "Flying High" out of construction paper.
7. Assemble the board as shown.

HOT-AIR BALLOON

28

FLOATING HIGH

Draw yourself in the balloon basket.
Then draw a picture of what you see as you float high above the earth.

HOW DOES THE WIND BLOW?

Let the children help to make a simple weather vane to use in observing the direction from which the wind is blowing.

What To Use:
drinking straw
string
pencil (with an eraser)
cardboard
straight pin
long stick

What To Do:
1. Cut an arrow out of lightweight cardboard.
2. Push a straight pin through the center of a drinking straw. Slit the straw and insert the cardboard arrow as shown.
3. Push the straight pin into the eraser of a pencil.
4. Tie the pencil to the end of a long stick.
5. Take the children outside on a windy day to observe the weather vane at work. Push the end of the stick into the ground and stand back to observe and discuss the changing direction of the wind.

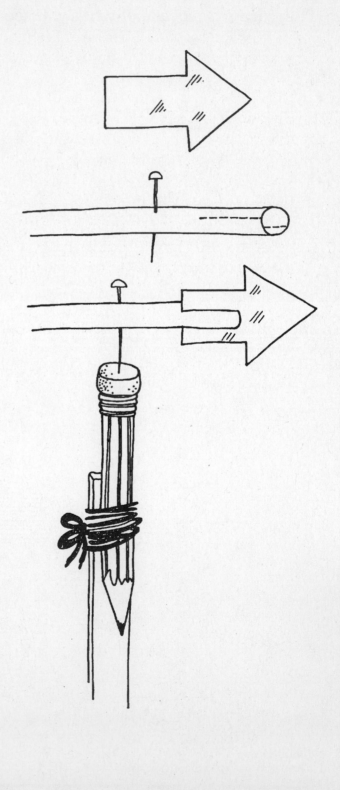

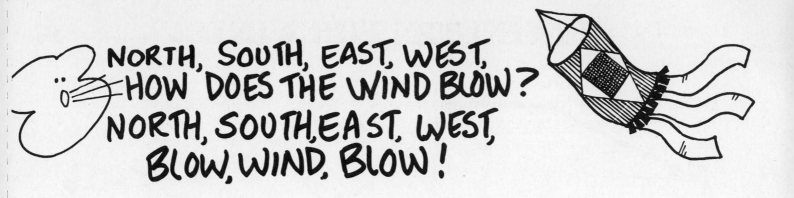

NORTH, SOUTH, EAST, WEST, HOW DOES THE WIND BLOW? NORTH, SOUTH, EAST, WEST, BLOW, WIND, BLOW!

Have the children play this game to reinforce their understanding of the directions north, south, east and west.

1. Have the children form a circle.
2. Ask one child to pretend to be the wind. Instruct the child to stand in the middle of the circle, with eyes closed, and to chant "north, south, east, west" as he or she points in each direction.
3. Whomever the wind is pointing to when "it" names the last direction becomes the wind and moves to the center of the circle.
4. Continue the game in this manner (with the children in the circle moving to the left after each turn) until each child has had the opportunity to be the wind.

FLYING ON THE WIND

KITE

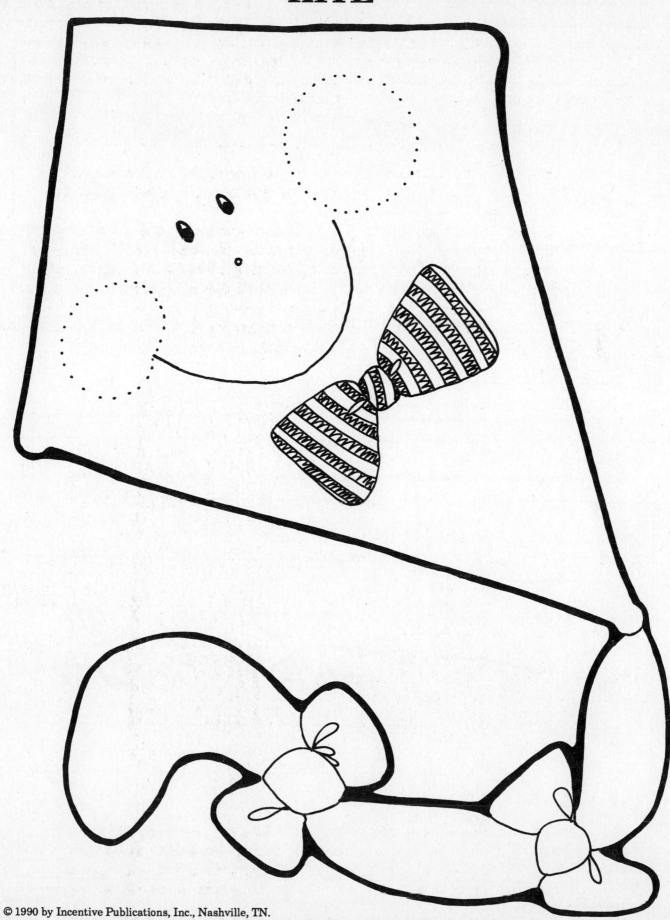

SELF-CONCEPT "INFLATORS"

_____

is up UP and away

with _____.

Signed _____

Date _____

is a flying-high
student because

_____

_____.

signed   date

LEAPING LEPRECHAUNS

Major Objective:
Children will develop awareness of and appreciation for the history, traditions and legends surrounding Saint Patrick's Day.

Things To Do:
- Show the children where Ireland is located on a world map or globe. Explain that St. Patrick's Day originated in Ireland and has remained an important holiday to people of Irish descent living all over the world. Discuss the symbols and traditions associated with St. Patrick's Day (shamrocks, leprechauns, Irish stew, soda bread, parades, etc.).

- Celebrate St. Patrick's Day by "displaying" as much green as possible. Ask the children to wear green and to bring a green toy, book or other object to class to share with the group. Write a list of "green things" on a chart and ask the children to suggest items to add to the list. Serve green lemonade, lime sherbert, lime Jell-O or cookies with green frosting for a snack.

- Reproduce the activities on pages 36 - 40 and have the children complete one activity each day during a given week. Have the children complete the "Leprechaun Hide & Seek" activity (page 36) at the end of the week and use it as a cover sheet for their work.

- Reproduce page 42 in quantities to meet the needs of the class. Help each child cut a shamrock out of green construction paper and string it on a strand of green yarn to make a necklace. Let the children wear their shamrock necklaces on March 17!

- Stage a St. Patrick's Day parade. Have the children wear their shamrock necklaces and sing, dance, and generally "make merry" through the classroom!

LEPRECHAUN HIDE AND SEEK

Find and circle 6 leprechauns in the picture.

Name _____ Date _____

Visual discrimination/counting
© 1990 by Incentive Publications, Inc., Nashville, TN.

Name _____

SOMETHING IS WRONG

Color everything in the pictures except the mistakes.
Make an X on every mistake.

Visual closure/finding mistakes
© 1990 by Incentive Publications, Inc., Nashville, TN.

Name _____

THE LEPRECHAUN'S PICNIC

Cut along the lines to make a puzzle.
Paste the puzzle pieces on another sheet of paper to put the leprechaun
picnic together again!

Visual closure/puzzles
© 1990 by Incentive Publications, Inc., Nashville, TN.

TOE-TICKLING LEPRECHAUNS

The leprechauns took off their shoes to tickle their toes in the grass.
Trace a path to help each leprechaun find his shoes.

Figure ground/maze
© 1990 by Incentive Publications, Inc., Nashville, TN.

MARCH MATCH-UPS

The picture in each box is part of another picture in that row.
Color the picture that shows the part.

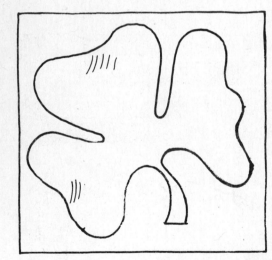 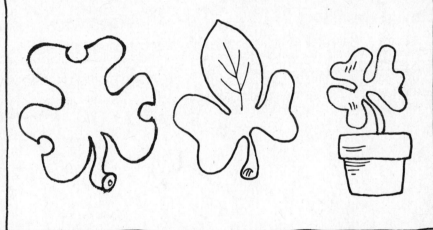

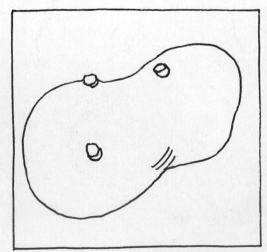 

SHAMROCK WREATH

Color and cut out the wreath.
Take it home to say "Happy St. Patrick's Day" to your family!

LUCK OF THE IRISH

Color and cut out the pencil toppers below.
Use them on your pencils for good luck!

CUT OUT

ST. PATRICK'S DAY

RECIPES FIT FOR A LEPRECHAUN

Tasty-Toasty Irish Soda Bread

4 cups flour (unsifted)
1 tsp. baking soda
2 tbs. sugar
1 tsp. salt
1 cup light (seedless) raisins
1 cup buttermilk

4 tbs. butter
large mixing bowl
measuring spoons & cup
cookie sheet
waxed paper
table knife

1. Mix flour, soda, sugar and salt in large bowl. Stir in raisins.
2. Make a well in center of mixture and pour in buttermilk. Stir until well blended.
3. Knead dough 8 to 10 times on floured wax paper. Roll dough into ball.
4. Use 1 1/2 tablespoons butter to grease cookie sheet. Place dough ball on cookie sheet and pat into thick circle.
5. Use floured table knife to make an X on top of loaf (keeps loaf from cracking). Use knife to spread remaining butter on top and sides of loaf.
6. Bake loaf in preheated oven (375°) approximately forty minutes. Check periodically to see if top of loaf is golden brown. Serve with butter and green mint jelly!

Leaping Leprechaun Jelly-O's

2 pkgs. unflavored gelatin
2 pkgs. lime gelatin
1 cup boiling water

2 cups cold water
1 tsp. cooking oil

1. Mix 2 packages unflavored gelatin with 1 cup cold water.
2. Stir 2 packages lime gelatin into 1 cup boiling water. Add to unflavored gelatin mixture.
3. Stir in 2 cups cold water.
4. Pour in oiled pan. Chill several hours or overnight.
5. Let kids use cookie cutters to cut favorite shapes. Remove shapes with a spatula and eat!

ACT IT OUT

- Children never tire of acting out nursery rhymes, finger plays or choral readings. Have the children act out the rhymes on page 53. Then work on building your own collection of rhymes. Copy or paste the rhymes on index cards and file them under subject headings.

- Use familiar stories as plays for the children to present. First, read or tell the story to the class. Then ask the children to pantomime the story or present the story using puppets or flannel board characters. You may want to assign speaking parts and have the children present the story in true play fashion. Depending on the maturity level of the class, you may want to read the narrative parts and have the children improvise their own speaking parts. After the group has had several experiences with the same story, you may give the narrator's part to a child.

- *Three Billy Goats Gruff* is an exciting story which will hold the interest of the total group (see pages 51 - 52). The children who do not have acting parts can clap the rhythm of the goats "tripping over the bridge" and can join in the singing of the goats' song. This story also works well as a flannel board activity for group presentations or independent free-time center use.

- *Goldilocks And The Three Bears* has been rewritten to give an old favorite a bit of contemporary flair and to provide short speaking parts that encourage spontaneous improvisation (see pages 58 - 59). Have the children draw pictures of their favorite parts of the story, make up scenes about "what happened next" to Goldilocks and the bears, and/or act out new situations involving their favorite characters.

- *The Three Little Pigs* is an all-time favorite of young children. Reproduce page 62 for each child and instruct the children to color, cut out and assemble the finger puppets. After the children "present" the story, let them take home their finger puppets and copies of the story (pages 60 - 61) to use in "family puppet plays"!

THREE BILLY GOATS GRUFF

Narrator: Early one morning, the three Billy Goats Gruff decided to climb to the top of the hillside where the grass was very green. So, they set out on the path leading across a bridge and up the hillside. Little did they know there was an ugly troll hiding under the bridge.

Three Billy Goats Gruff: (Sung to the tune of *Here We Go 'Round The Mulberry Bush*.)
Three Billy Goat Brothers are we, are we
Our stomachs are empty as can be,
Green grass sweet
Is what we'll eat
'Till we're as fat as can be.

Troll: Who's that singing and tripping across my bridge?

Little Billy Goat Gruff: It's only I, Little Billy Goat Gruff. I'm on my way to the green, grassy hilltop to eat and get fat (spoken in a tiny voice).

Troll: You've disturbed my nap! I'm going to gobble you up!

Little Billy Goat Gruff: Please don't gobble me up. I wouldn't make even half-a-mouthful. My brother is right behind me. He is much bigger than I and will make a better meal for you.

Troll: Well, all right. Now get off my bridge and be on your way!

Narrator: Just then Middle-sized Billy Goat Gruff came to the bridge.

Middle-sized Billy Goat Gruff: (Sings song as he crosses the bridge.)

Troll: Who's that singing and tripping across my bridge?

Middle-sized Billy Goat Gruff: It's only I, Middle-sized Billy Goat Gruff. I'm on my way to the green, grassy hilltop to eat and get fat.

Troll: Your brother disturbed my nap. I've been waiting for you. I'm going to gobble you up!

Middle-sized Billy Goat Gruff: Please don't gobble me up. I'm just a middle-sized goat, but my big brother is right behind me. He will make a much better meal!

Troll: Well, all right. Now get off my bridge and be on your way!

Narrator: Just then Big Billy Goat Gruff came to the bridge.

Big Billy Goat Gruff: (Sings song as he crosses the bridge.)

Troll: Who's that singing and tripping across my bridge?

Big Billy Goat Gruff: It's I, Big Billy Goat Gruff. I'm on my way to the green, grassy hilltop to eat and get fat (spoken in a very gruff voice).

Troll: Your brothers have kept me from my nap. I'm going to gobble you up!

Big Billy Goat Gruff: Just you try! I'll use my horns to throw you off this bridge!

Narrator: And that's just what Big Billy Goat Gruff did. The three Billy Goats Gruff sang all the way to the top of the grassy hillside, and the troll was never seen again!

LITTLE BILLY GOAT GRUFF

MIDDLE-SIZED BILLY GOAT GRUFF

BIG BILLY GOAT GRUFF

TROLL AND BRIDGE

THREE BILLY GOATS GRUFF SCENERY

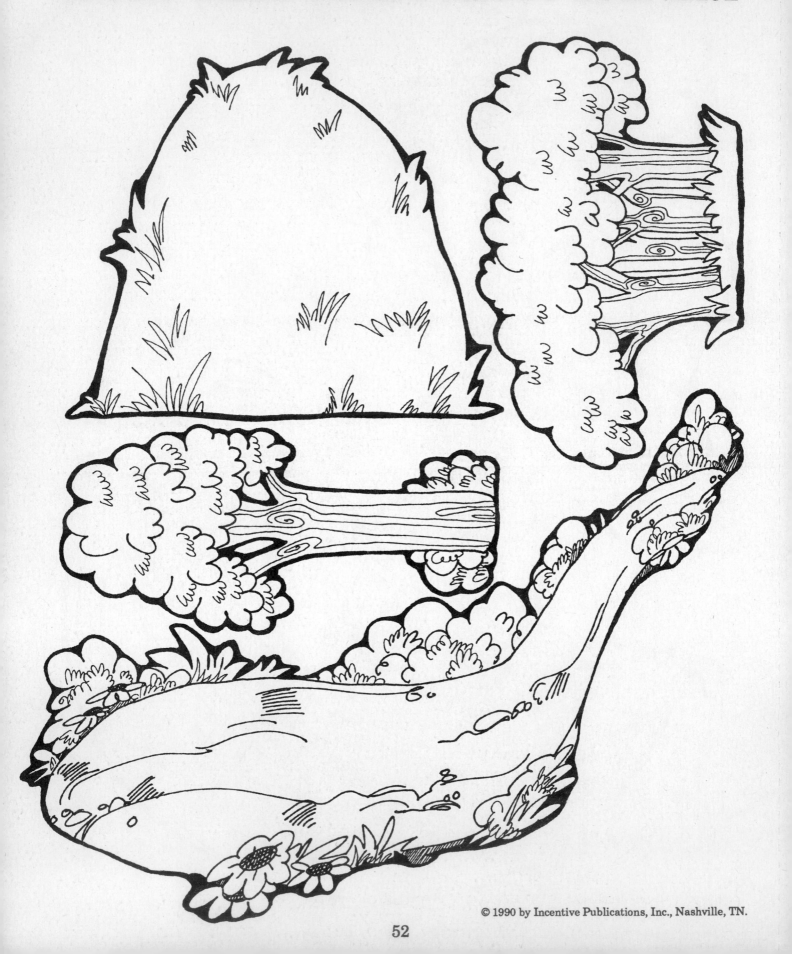

RHYMES TO ACT OUT

Jack be nimble,
Jack be quick,
Jack jump over
The candle stick.

Jack and Jill
Went up the hill
To fetch a pail of water;
Jack fell down
And broke his crown
And Jill came tumbling after.

Little Jack Horner
Sat in a corner
Eating his Christmas pie;
He stuck in his thumb
And pulled out a plum
And said, "What a good boy
    am I!"

GOLDILOCKS AND THE THREE BEARS

Narrator: Long ago in a faraway land lived a pleasant and curious little girl named Goldilocks. Across the village lived three bears. One morning Papa Bear made some porridge for breakfast, but the porridge was too hot to eat. So, the bears decided to take a walk while the porridge cooled. Just then Goldilocks was taking her morning walk. She came upon the bear's cottage and noticed that the door was cracked. She decided to go inside and make some new friends. When she saw that no one was there, she decided to wait for them to return. She sat down in Mama Bear's chair and tasted her porridge.

Goldilocks: This porridge is too hot.

Narrator: Next she tried Papa Bear's porridge.

Goldilocks: This porridge is too lumpy.

Narrator: Then she tried Baby Bear's porridge.

Goldilocks: This porridge is just right!

Narrator: And she ate it all up. Then she went upstairs and climbed into Papa Bear's bed.

Goldilocks: This bed is too hard.

Narrator: Then she tried Mama Bear's bed.

Goldilocks: This bed is too soft.

Narrator: Then she tried Baby Bear's bed.

Goldilocks: This bed is just right!

Narrator:	And she fell fast asleep. Soon the bears returned from their walk and sat down at the table. Papa bear noticed that his spoon had been moved.
Papa Bear:	Someone's been eating my porridge.
Mama Bear:	Someone's been eating my porridge, too!
Baby Bear:	Someone's been eating my porridge, and it's all gone!
Narrator:	Baby Bear began to cry, so Mama Bear put more porridge on to cook and they all went upstairs to rest. Papa Bear looked at his bed and said...
Papa Bear:	Someone's been sleeping in my bed.
Mama Bear:	Someone's been sleeping in my bed, too.
Baby Bear:	Someone's been sleeping in my bed, and she's still there!
Narrator:	Just then Goldilocks woke up and saw the bears. She jumped out of bed, bowed to the bears and, because she was a pleasant child, said...
Goldilocks:	Please excuse me! I meant no harm. I hope that we can be friends!
Narrator:	So, the three bears asked Goldilocks to stay and they became friends. Ever since that day, Goldilocks has stopped by the bear's cottage each morning as she takes her walk to say hello to her good friends.

THE THREE LITTLE PIGS

Narrator: Once upon a time in a faraway land there lived a mother pig and her three little pigs. One day the mother pig called the little pigs to her side and said...

Mother Pig: It's time for you to build houses of your own. It won't be easy, but the big world out there you will see.

Narrator: So, the three little pigs left home to build houses of their own. The first little pig built a house of straw. The second little pig built a house of sticks. The third little pig built a house of bricks. One day, the big bad wolf came upon the straw house that belonged to the first little pig.

Big Bad Wolf: Hmmm. A little pig would make a good lunch! (Knock, knock, knock.) Little pig, little pig, let me come in!

Little Pig 1: Not by the hair of my chinny-chin-chin!

Big Bad Wolf: Then I'll huff and I'll puff and I'll blow your house down!

Narrator: So, he huffed and he puffed and he blew the house down. But the first little pig got out the back way and ran to the house of the second little pig. The next day the big bad wolf came upon the house of sticks that belonged to the second little pig.

Big Bad Wolf: (Knock, knock, knock.) Little pig, little pig, let me come in!

Little Pig 2: Not by the hair of my chinny-chin-chin!

Big Bad Wolf: Then I'll huff and I'll puff and I'll blow your house down!

Narrator: So he huffed and he puffed and he blew the house down. But the little pigs got out the back way and ran to the house of the third little pig. The next day, the big bad wolf came upon the brick house that belonged to the third little pig.

Big Bad Wolf: (Knock, knock, knock.) Little pig, little pig, let me come in!

Little Pig 3: Not by the hair of my chinny-chin-chin!

Big Bad Wolf: Then I'll huff and I'll puff and I'll blow your house down!

Narrator: So he huffed and he puffed, and he huffed and he puffed, but he could not blow down the brick house.

Big Bad Wolf: Little pig, I'm going to climb onto your roof and come down the chimney. Then I'm going to eat you up!

Little Pig 3: Go ahead and try it!

Narrator: So, the wolf climbed onto the roof. But the third little pig lit a fire in the fireplace and put a pot of water on to boil. The wolf slid down the chimney and landed in the pot. He huffed and he puffed until he climbed out of the pot, and then he ran out the door as fast as he could. Needless to say, the three little pigs have never seen the wolf again!

THREE LITTLE PIGS FINGER PUPPETS

Color and cut out the finger puppets.
Tape the puppets together and act out the story.

PANTOMIME

Pantomiming helps even the shyest child "feel" a situation and experience an emotion without imposing undue stress upon the child. It also helps to build confidence for further involvement in group activities and creative projects.

Ask the children to pantomime simple one-step activities in a group setting.

1. Fly a kite on a very windy day.
2. Walk in wet sand or mud.
3. Blow out candles on a birthday cake.
4. Brush your hair or your teeth.
5. Throw a ball into a basketball net.
6. Eat a juicy piece of watermelon.
7. Hop like a toad.
8. Drink soda from a bottle.
9. Build a sand castle.
10. Carry a tiny baby.

Next, move to two or three-step activities.
1. Pick apples from a tree and put them in a basket.
2. Put on your socks and then your shoes.
3. Open an envelope and read the letter.
4. Get into a car and close the door.
5. Cut a piece of meat and eat it.
6. Slice a piece of cake, put it on a plate and serve it to someone.
7. Take your coat off of a hanger and put it on.
8. Pour milk into a glass, drink the milk and put the glass on a table.
9. Answer the door, invite the visitor to come in, and close the door.
10. Unwrap a birthday package and take the gift out of the box.

Name _____

JUST PRETENDING

Pretend that you can be anything or anyone you want to be for one day.
Draw a picture of who or what you will be.

Imaging/visualizing
© 1990 by Incentive Publications, Inc., Nashville, TN.

PRETENDING

Isn't it wonderful that by pretending children can be anything or anyone they want to be? In addition to providing children with fun experiences, the act of pretending helps children to develop skills in:

- self-expression
- creating, composing and interpreting
- responding to songs, stories and poetry

- creative drama
- rhythm and body movements
- and, most importantly, self-awareness and personal esteem

Begin group pretending experiences by giving simple directions such as those below:

Pretend to be . . .

1. a tree on a high hill on a windy day.

2. a snowman beginning to melt.
3. a bird with an injured wing trying to fly.
4. a cloud in the sky on a bright, sunny day.

5. walking barefoot in spring grass.

6. a goldfish swimming in a fishbowl.

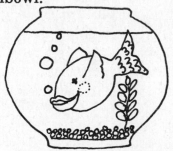

7. a very old lady walking with a cane.
8. a baby just learning to eat with a spoon.

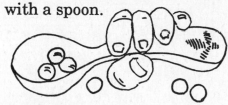

9. riding a bicycle up a hill.
10. walking in shoes that are too small for your feet.

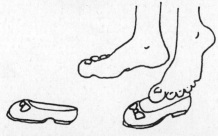

11. a sailboat on a windy sea.
12. an old, ragged teddy bear in the bottom of a toy chest.

Now the children should be ready to pantomime situations involving emotions that require more self-expression. Ask one child at a time to act out the situations below and to conclude each with an original ending.

1. You are carrying a cup of very hot tea to your mother. Suddenly, your dog dashes into the room and runs directly into you. He yaps and nips at your legs, begging you to play with him. You...

2. You are standing on an ice-covered pond. Suddenly, you feel the ice begin to break under you and...

3. You awaken in the middle of the night to the sound of a loud noise. You jump out of bed and rush to the door to find someone standing in the doorway with a flash light in hand. When you try to run past the person, you...

4. The phone rings. You answer it and your best friend invites you to go to a movie you want to see. You ask your mother for permission to go and she says that you cannot go because your grandmother is coming to visit. So, you...

5. You are standing on a chair holding a breakable toy you have just taken off the top shelf. When the chair begins to sway, you...

After several children have had time to pantomime the same situations, adding their own original endings, discuss the performances and compare the various endings.

IT'S OUR WORLD

Major Objective:
Children will develop awareness of the earth's natural resources and of the need to preserve, protect and replenish these resources.

Things To Do:

- Because March 21 is Earth Day and March 19-25 is National Wildlife Week, March is the perfect time to introduce children to ecology. For information and materials related to wildlife and the earth's natural resources, write to:

  The National Wildlife Federation
  1412 16th St. N.W.
  Washington, D.C. 20036

- Take walks around the school grounds and help the children look for plants and animals in their natural habitats. Ask questions to stimulate discussion. Make a list of the plants and animals sighted and their characteristics. Place picture books on the reading table for follow-up and reinforcement activities.

- Take a "listening walk." Ask the children to sit or stand, to close their eyes and to listen to the sounds around them. Help them to distinguish between man-made sounds and nature's sounds. As a follow-up, have the children complete page 71.

- Set aside one day for "ecology day." Discuss the meaning of the word ecology. Reproduce page 74 in quantities to meet the needs of the class. Have the children color and cut out the emblems. Ask each child to select two people who are good "ecologists" and to present the awards to them. Have the children take turns explaining why these people deserve the awards. Ask the children to wear the wrist band home and to discuss the message with family members.

- Reproduce page 65 in quantities to meet the needs of the class. Have the children complete and color the poster. Save the children's completed activities (pages 68-72) and compile them to make take-home booklets. Use the children's posters as booklet covers for their work.

- Take a walk around school grounds to collect litter. Remind the children to pick up only items that are safe to handle (no broken glass, objects with jagged edges, etc.). Take the litter back to the classroom and help the children arrange and paste the litter on a large sheet of construction paper to make a collage. Write the following on the collage: "Look what we found. Please help us keep our school litter free!" Post the collage in the hall to encourage other classes to join in your "clean up campaign."

- Demonstrate the balance of nature by helping the children construct a vivarium for the science table. You will need the following materials:

  - large glass container (over-sized pickle jar or fish bowl, etc.)
  - piece of screen wire (to cover the container)
  - small bowl (to hold water for the animals)
  - small pebbles (to line the bottom of the container)
  - soil (to cover the pebbles)
  - 2 or 3 small pieces of charcoal (to keep the air clean)
  - plants and animals

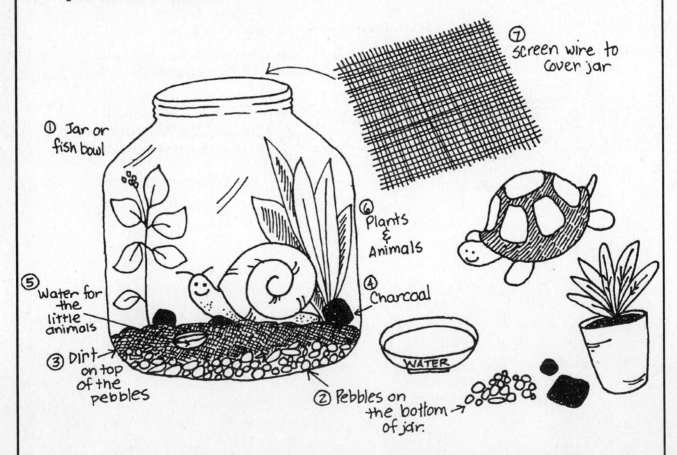

Turtles, snails and insects are good animal choices. Regardless of what animals you choose, remember to return them to their natural environments after a few days. Tell the children that, just like boys and girls, the animals can visit other environments, but home is the best place of all!

My name is _____ .

I am part of a great big world!

WE ALL LIVE TOGETHER MOBILE

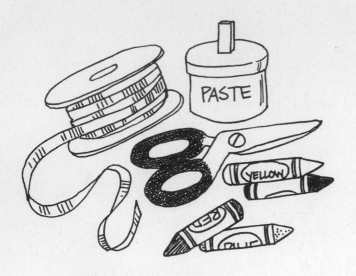

What To Use:
ribbon
paste
scissors
crayons

What To Do:
1. Reproduce the patterns on page 67 in quantities to meet the needs of the class.
2. Have each child color and cut out a set of patterns.
3. Help the children paste their patterns on strands of ribbon as shown to make mobiles.
4. Hang the mobiles from the ceiling, the children's desks or classroom windows.

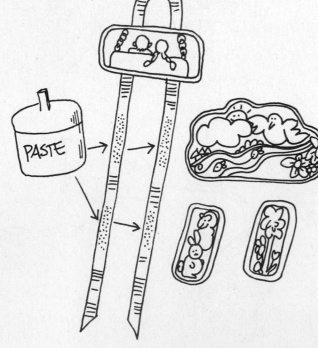

MOBILE PATTERNS

Name _____

POLLUTION IN OUR NEIGHBORHOOD

People need clean air, water and space in order to live and grow.
We say that unclean air, water or space is polluted.
Draw a picture of something that causes pollution in your neighborhood.

Environmental awareness/pollution
© 1990 by Incentive Publications, Inc., Nashville, TN.

UNCLEAN AIR

Make a red X on pictures of 5 things that cause air pollution.
Color the rest of the picture.

WATER FOR LIFE

People cannot live without fresh water.
Sometimes we forget to protect our fresh water supply.
Color and cut out the checklist below.
Take it home to remind you and your family not to
    waste or pollute water.

I do not let water run
unnecessarily.   _____

I do not throw bottles and
cans in lakes, rivers or streams.   _____

I do not put things that do not dissolve
easily down the drain.   _____

I will remind others to help protect
our fresh water supply.   _____

Name _____   Date _____

Environmental awareness/water pollution
© 1990 by Incentive Publications, Inc., Nashville, TN.

DON'T PITCH IT, RECYCLE IT!

Recycling is a big word.
It means using something again in another way.
Color the pictures of things that can be recycled.
Take this poster home and discuss with your family things you can recycle.

NEWSPAPERS

GLASS

TIN CANS

ALUMINUM CANS

Environmental awareness/recycling
© 1990 by Incentive Publications, Inc., Nashville, TN.

LABEL A LITTER BAG

Color and cut out the litter bag label below.
Paste it on a sturdy paper bag.
Take your litter bag with you on your next family trip!

MARKERS FOR REMINDERS

Color and cut out the bookmarks below.
Keep one for yourself and give 2 bookmarks to family members as reminders to protect our natural wildlife.

Environmental awareness/natural wildlife
© 1990 by Incentive Publications, Inc., Nashville, TN.

ECOLOGY REMINDERS

1. Cut out the wrist band.
2. Fold along the dotted lines.
3. Cut where indicated and assemble the wrist band around the child's arm.

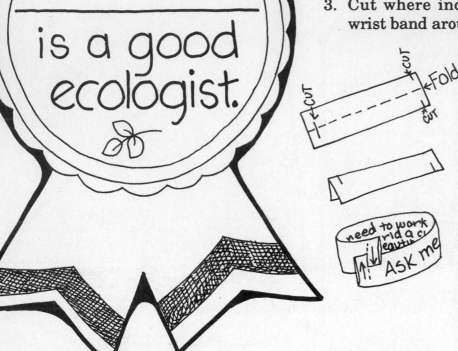

_____ is a good ecologist.

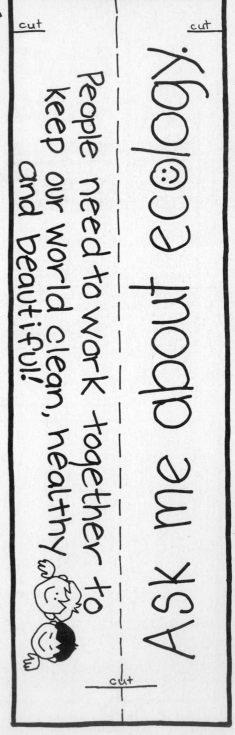

People need to work together to keep our world clean, healthy and beautiful!

Ask me about ecology.

_____ works to keep the air clean, the water pure, and the world a healthy place to live.

GROW A GARBAGE CAN GARDEN

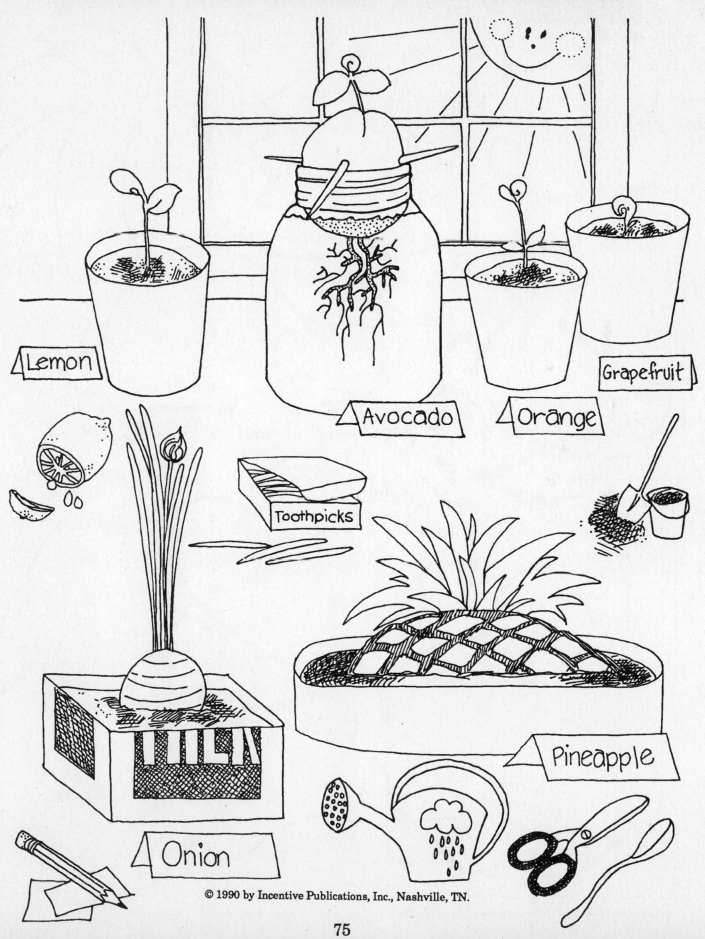

Lemon

Avocado

Orange

Grapefruit

Toothpicks

Onion

Pineapple

WILDLIFE

ECOLOGIST'S DOORKNOB DECORATION

Color and cut out this doorknob decoration.
Hang it on your door to tell the world that you are a good ecologist!

CUT OUT
CENTER
AND
SLASH ON
DOTTED
LINES

we are good
ecologists.
We respect and
protect our natural
wildlife.

BIBLIOGRAPHY

The Day They Parachuted Cats On Dorneo: A Drama of Ecology. Charlotte Pomerantz. Yound Scott Books, Addison-Wesley.
   This play based on an actual event reported in *The New York Times* contains good poems about ecology and the study of living things.

Earth. Alfred Leutscher. Dial Press.
   The colorful and realistic artwork in this book describes the earth below us.

Gilberto and the Wind. Marie Hall Ets. Viking Press.
   An imaginative little boy enjoys playing in the wind until both he and the wind fall asleep.

The Hidden Life of the Forest; The Hidden Life of the Meadow; The Hidden Life of the Pond. David Schwartz. Crown Publishers.
   These books have appropriate texts and beautiful illustrations for the study of nature.

How the Wind Blows. Katherine D. Marks. Abingdon Press.
   This book is a "description in words and illustrations" of how moving air becomes wind and how wind affects our lives.

I Can Be a Weather Forecaster. Claire Martin. Children's Press.
   This introduction to weather forecasting includes a full-color picture dictionary.

Life and Death in Nature. Seymour Simon. McGraw-Hill.
   This book will help children understand the ecological cycle of plants and animals.

The Little Witch's Spring Holiday Book. Linda Glovach. Prentice Hall.
   This book is packed with lots of fun and creative things to make and do.

Mirandy and Brother Wind. Patricia C. McKissack. Alfred A. Knopf.
   The delightful illustrations in this book present the cake walk, a dance rooted in Afro-American culture, as a "dance with the wind."

Mother Goose Learning Fun. Imogene Forte. Incentive Publications.
   Favorite Mother Goose rhymes are accompanied by stand-up figures and fun activities to reinforce early skills.

Spring Green. Valerie M. Selkowe. Lothrop, Lee & Shepard.
   Woody Wood Chuck offers a prize for the best green thing brought to his spring party. The prize-winning green thing gives the book a surprise ending!

St. Patrick's Day. Mary Cantwell. Thomas Y. Crowell Co.
   This book conveys St. Patrick's life and "explains" St. Patrick's Day.

Take a Trip to Ireland. Dan James. Franklin Watts Co.
   This "photographic journey" through Ireland contains simple geographical and historical notes.

This is Ireland. Miroslav Sasek. Fabbristampa.
   This book about Ireland, its customs and its people is filled with whimsical illustrations that add sparkle to the observance of St. Patrick's Day.

Weather. Terri Jennings. Glouscester Press.
   This book contains activities and experiments for learning about the weather.

INDEX